Machu Picchu

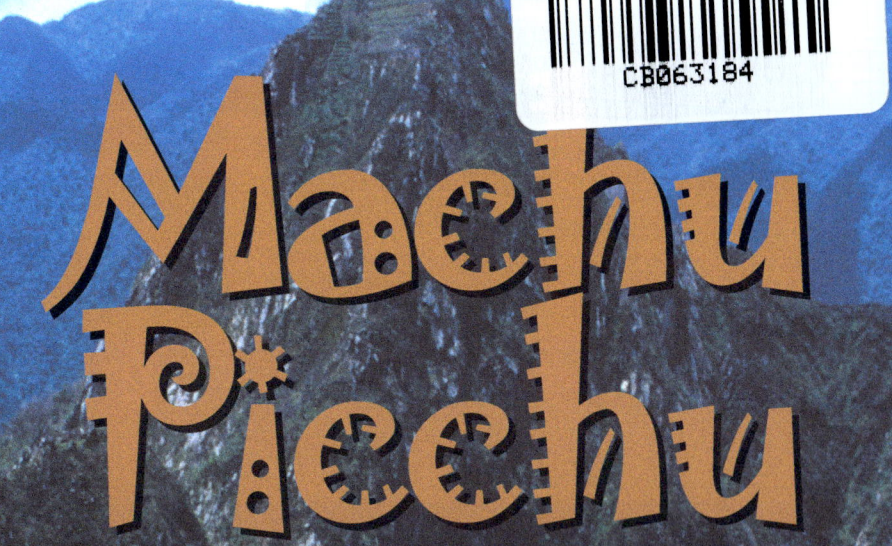

Machu Picchu	2
Where is Machu Picchu?	4
Who discovered Machu Picchu?	5
What does Machu Picchu look like?	6
Who lived at Machu Picchu?	8
History	10
Story: Through the Fence	11
Activities	27
Bilingual Dictionary	31

Original text by Murray Pile
Retold by Maria Toth

Machu Picchu

Machu Picchu is an old Inca city in Peru in South America. The great conqueror and builder Pachacuti Inca probably built the city in the 15th century. The Incas were native South American people and they ruled a big empire on the west coast of South America.

The Incas abandoned Machu Picchu some time in the 16th century. Hiram Bingham, an American explorer, rediscovered the Lost City of Machu Picchu in 1911.

3

Where is Machu Picchu?

Machu Picchu is very high up in the Andes Mountains in Peru. It is about 80 kilometres northwest of Cuzco. It is 2,134 metres above sea level between two big mountains. The Urubamba river lies at the bottom of the valley between the two mountains. Machu Picchu covers an area of about 13 square kilometres.

South America

Who discovered Machu Picchu?

Hiram Bingham discovered Machu Picchu in 1911. He was a teacher at the Yale University in the USA. When he arrived at Machu Picchu, there was jungle everywhere. He worked very hard to uncover the city. People were amazed by the size and magnificence of the Lost City of the Incas.

A photo of Machu Picchu taken by Hiram Bingham (above).

What does Machu Picchu look like?

The Incas built the city on terraces and there were hundreds of stairs and paths connecting the terraces. The paths also connected open spaces called *plazas*, houses and a cemetery.

Machu Picchu is a terraced city.

The Incas built their houses from big pieces of stone. The stone is called granite. The large pieces of stone fit tightly together. Most of the stone houses have one room.

Who lived at Machu Picchu?

People are not sure about the history of Machu Picchu. About 1,200 Inca people lived in and around Machu Picchu and most of them were women, children and priests.

Some people think the royal family lived in Machu Picchu when they were not in the main city of Cuzco. Some of the buildings look like houses for farmers and servants of the royal family.

Other people think that Machu Picchu was an important religious city because there are many shrines and temples.

A street in Cuzco today.

Native women today on the terraces of Machu Picchu.

History

We think the Incas left the great city of Machu Picchu in the middle of the 16th century. Spanish soldiers, called *conquistadors*, arrived in the Inca Empire at this time too, looking for treasure to take back to Spain. But the Spanish probably did not find Machu Picchu because it was too high in the mountains and it was difficult to reach.

After the Incas abandoned their city, jungle grew all over the buildings. It was a lost city until it was rediscovered in 1911.

Today, the lost city of Machu Picchu is a world famous tourist attraction. Many people travel to Machu Picchu to see the ruins of the city and walk along the Inca Trail, which goes from Cuzco to Machu Picchu. There are also other lost Inca cities in the area of Machu Picchu.

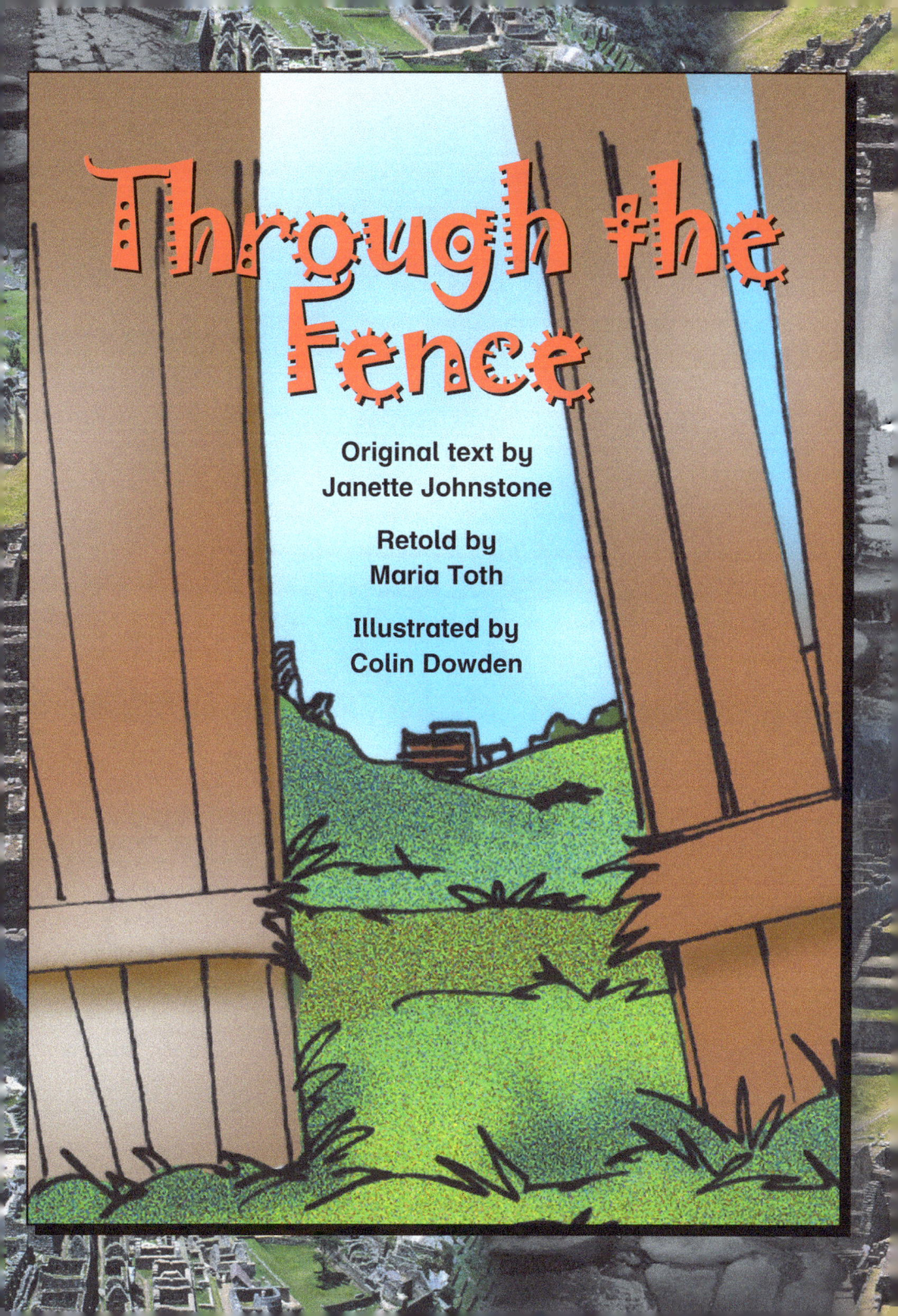

Through the Fence

Original text by Janette Johnstone

Retold by Maria Toth

Illustrated by Colin Dowden

It was a warm afternoon. Abby, Sam and Josh were on holiday from school and they were bored.

"What are we going to do?" asked Josh.

"Why don't we go skateboarding in the park?" said Sam.

"That isn't very exciting," said Abby. "I know! Why don't we go exploring?"

"That's a good idea, but where can we go?" asked Sam.

"Well, we can explore the old house next to the park. It's very spooky," said Abby.

"OK, let's go!" said Sam.

So the three friends went quickly down the stairs to the street and across the park to the old house. It had a high fence.

"Look, there's a hole in the fence. Let's climb through it!" Abby said. "Come on!"

Abby climbed through the hole first and she disappeared. Then Sam followed her. Josh felt nervous on his own and didn't know what to do.

So Josh decided to follow the others. He climbed slowly through the hole in the fence. He caught his yellow shorts on a nail in the fence. So he pushed and pushed hard with his feet.

Suddenly he started to fall and he closed his eyes tight. Everything went black. He was in a tunnel going down and down.

When Josh opened his eyes he was sitting on a rock next to Abby and Sam. They weren't in the garden of the old house; they were in the middle of some mountains.

"Where are we? How did we get here?" asked Josh.

"I don't know. We're somewhere in the mountains," replied Abby. "We must be really high up because we can nearly touch the clouds."

"Look!" said Sam, "There's a big city up there and there are some stone steps in the mountain!"
"Come on, let's explore!" said Abby.

"There's a boy at the top of the steps," said Abby. "Let's go and talk to him."
So the three friends walked up the steps to the boy. He was tall with straight dark hair and dark eyes. He had a long stick in his hand.

"Hello," said Abby, "We're lost. Who are you? What's your name?"
"My name's Titu. Titu is also the name of a famous Inca chief. I live in this city," he said, pointing at the city in the mountains. "It's called Machu Picchu."
"I read about Machu Picchu at school," said Sam. "It was a lost Inca city. I think we're back in the time of the Incas. We're in the past!"
"Where do you come from? How did you get here?" asked Titu.
"We come from a big city in England. We went to an old house and climbed through a hole in the fence and I think we went back in time," said Abby.

Titu asked many questions and Abby, Sam and Josh tried to answer them. Abby, Sam and Josh asked lots of questions too. They wanted to know about Machu Picchu. Titu loved his city, but he was afraid. The Spanish conquistadors had a camp in the valley below the city. The soldiers didn't find Machu Picchu but they captured Titu's sister. Titu was on his way to rescue her. She was in the Spanish camp next to the Urubamba River in the valley.

"Can we come with you?" asked Sam.

"Yes, we can help you," said Abby.

"Thank you," said Titu. "It's a long way down the mountain and a difficult journey. Hurry!"

Sam and Abby followed Titu down the mountain. Josh was behind them but he was scared. Suddenly, Titu stopped and put his finger to his lips.

"We're near the Spanish camp now, so be very quiet," he whispered.

"Look," whispered Abby. "Is that your sister, tied to the tree?"

"Yes," said Titu. "That's Juana."

There were five soldiers next to Juana. Juana looked very small and very frightened. The soldiers had red trousers, brown boots, metal helmets and they had weapons. They weren't friendly!

"I've got a plan," said Abby. "Listen!"

Quickly and quietly, Titu went to the soldiers' horses and untied them.

"What's that noise?" asked one of the soldiers.

"Where are the horses?" asked another soldier and they started to run.

"Look! A boy! Come on. Let's catch him!" said one of the soldiers and they chased after Titu and the horses.

Abby and Sam ran to the tree and cut the rope around Juana's body. Josh looked out for the soldiers. "Don't be scared, Juana," said Abby. "We're here with your brother. Be very quiet and come with us. Do you understand?"

Juana looked at Abby and smiled. Then Josh whistled to Sam and Abby. "Quick! The soldiers are coming back!" They all ran away from the tree.

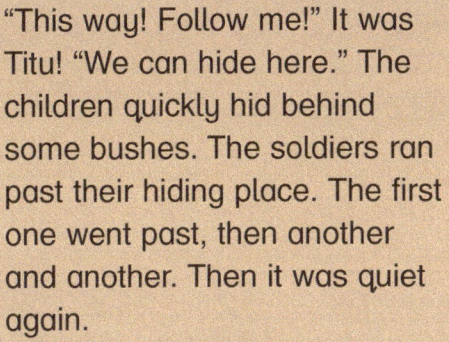

"This way! Follow me!" It was Titu! "We can hide here." The children quickly hid behind some bushes. The soldiers ran past their hiding place. The first one went past, then another and another. Then it was quiet again.
"What are we going to do now?" asked Josh.
"When it's night time, we can climb up the mountain back to Machu Picchu," said Titu.
So they waited until it was dark and then they climbed back up the mountain.

They walked all night and arrived in Machu Picchu in the morning. They were very tired but the people were so happy to see Juana again. They were heroes!

"I think this is where your adventure started," said Titu. "Goodbye my new friends!"

"Goodbye!" said Juana. "Thank you for rescuing me."

"Goodbye!" said Abby, Sam and Josh. They crawled into the hole in the mountain.

25

Abby, Sam and Josh crawled through a long, dark tunnel for a very long time. Suddenly they saw sunlight ahead and they climbed out of the tunnel. Then they saw the old house and the hole in the fence.
"What a brilliant adventure!" said Sam and Josh.
"Where are we going to go tomorrow?" Abby smiled.
"Nowhere!" answered Sam and Josh and they all laughed.

Activities

1 Circle T (True) or F (False).

1 Machu Picchu is in the Andes Mountains in Peru.   (T) F
2 Hiram Bingham discovered the city in 1913.   T F
3 It's on the east coast of South America.   T F
4 The ruins are 18 square kilometres.   T F
5 The city has hundreds of stairs and paths.   T F
6 The native South American people made houses from stone.   T F
7 The people left the city in the 17th century.   T F
8 Many tourists visit Machu Picchu every year.   T F

2 Complete the puzzle.

Across
3 Some people think Machu Picchu was a religious ...
6 There were paths, plazas, a cemetery and ...
7 Today, Machu Picchu is a tourist ...
8 The people who lived in Machu Picchu were ...
9 The Incas made their houses from ...

Down
1 The Urubamba is the name of a ...
2 The Incas built the city on ...
4 The Spanish did not find Machu Picchu because it was high in the ...
5 Machu Picchu is in ...

3 across: c i t y

3 Match the beginnings and endings of the sentences.

1 Hiram Bingham   many paths and terraces in the city.
2 Machu Picchu is 2,134 metres   in the valley below Machu Picchu.
3 The Incas made the houses   discovered the lost city in 1911.
4 There are   to see the ruins.
5 The river Urubamba is   above sea level.
6 Many tourists go to Machu Picchu   from stone.

4 Now match the sentences to the pictures by writing a number in each box.

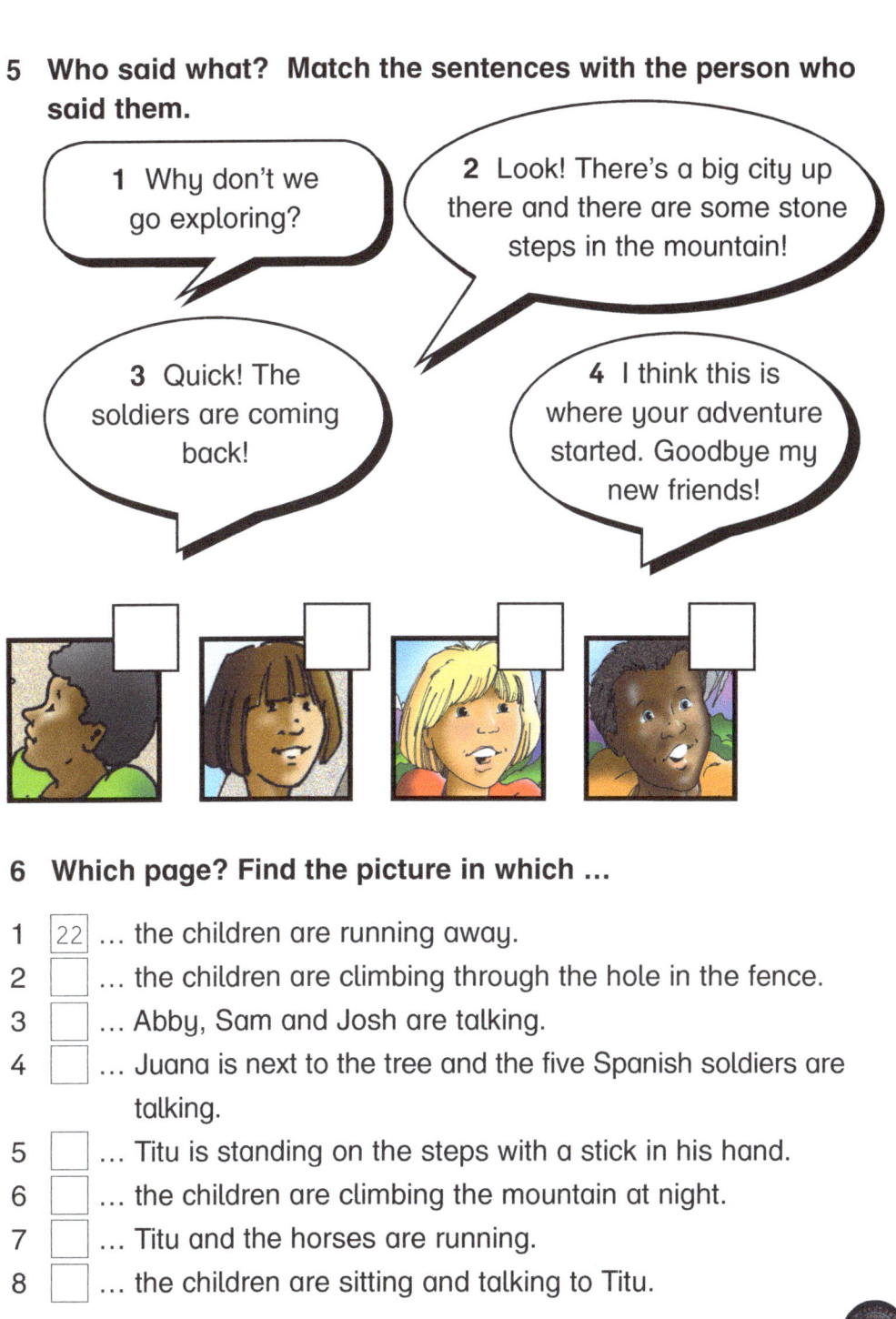

5 Who said what? Match the sentences with the person who said them.

1 Why don't we go exploring?

2 Look! There's a big city up there and there are some stone steps in the mountain!

3 Quick! The soldiers are coming back!

4 I think this is where your adventure started. Goodbye my new friends!

6 Which page? Find the picture in which …

1 [22] … the children are running away.
2 [ ] … the children are climbing through the hole in the fence.
3 [ ] … Abby, Sam and Josh are talking.
4 [ ] … Juana is next to the tree and the five Spanish soldiers are talking.
5 [ ] … Titu is standing on the steps with a stick in his hand.
6 [ ] … the children are climbing the mountain at night.
7 [ ] … Titu and the horses are running.
8 [ ] … the children are sitting and talking to Titu.

7 Complete the story with the words in the box.

Abby, Sam and Josh decide to go exploring. They go to the old (1) _house_ next to the park and climb through a hole in the (2) _____ . They go back in time and suddenly they find themselves in the middle of the (3) _____ next to Machu Picchu. The children meet Titu and Titu tells them he wants to (4)_____ his sister, Juana, from the Spanish (5) _____ . Abby has a (6) _____ . Titu unties the (7) _____ and Abby, Sam and Josh rescue Juana. They escape from the soldiers and then they (8) _____ back to Machu Picchu at night. Titu and the children say (9) _____ . Abby, Sam and Josh (10) _____ through the hole in the fence and arrive home again.

go	plan	climb	horses
fence	soldiers	goodbye	~~house~~
	mountains	rescue	

Bilingual Dictionary

Write the words in your language.

answer	_____	priest	_____
ask	_____	reach	_____
bored	_____	rediscovered	_____
camp	_____	religious	_____
catch	_____	rescue	_____
cemetery	_____	rope	_____
century	_____	ruins	_____
climb	_____	scared	_____
cover	_____	sea level	_____
cut	_____	servant	_____
dark	_____	shrine	_____
disappeared	_____	smile	_____
empire	_____	step	_____
farmer	_____	stick	_____
fence	_____	stone	_____
helmet	_____	terrace	_____
hide	_____	tired	_____
hole	_____	treasure	_____
horse	_____	untie	_____
know	_____	valley	_____
lips	_____	weapon	_____
lost	_____	west	_____
native	_____	whisper	_____
noise	_____	whistle	_____
nowhere	_____	women	_____
path	_____		

Macmillan Education
4 Crinan Street
London N1 9XW
A division of Macmillan Publishers Limited
Companies and representatives throughout the world

ISBN 978 1 4050 2512 6
ISBN 978 1 4050 5725 7 (International Edition)

Text © Macmillan Publishers Limited 2005
Design and illustration © Macmillan Publishers Limited 2005

First published 2005

All rights reserved; no part of this publication may be reproduced, stored in a retrieval system, transmitted in any form, or by any means, electronic, mechanical, photocopying, recording, or otherwise, without the prior written permission of the publishers.

Illustrated by Colin Dowden
Designed by Marion James Design

The authors and publishers would like to thank the following for permission to reproduce the following photographic material:

Cover photo Getty Images

Title page by Photodisc

Auscape International p6 ©Brian Vikander; Australian Picture Library pp6(inset), 9, 28(tl); Robert Harding Picture Library p28(br); National Geographic pp5(inset) ©Erdis, (main) ©Bingham, 28(r) ©Erdis; South American Picture Library pp8, 28(bl); Stone/Getty Images pp2/3, 6/7(main), 28(tm).

Royalty-free: pp10, 11, 28(bm) ©Photodisc

Printed and bound in Great Britain by Ashford Colour Press Ltd